Time Management

Mastering Time: Revealing The Strategies For Maximum Efficiency And Success With Time Management Techniques

(Optimizing Time Management And Increasing Daily Productivity)

Stefan BallardCrawford

TABLE OF CONTENT

Knowing What Productivity Is 1

What Evernote Can Do For You 8

Time Management Is A Requirement Of Leadership 19

Make Sure You Have A Proper Daily Strategy Before You Begin Each Morning. 53

Orient Yourself To Succeed 67

Setting Up Your Objectives 86

The Value Of Effective Time Management 93

Evaluating How Much Time You Spend Now 101

The Time Concept 115

Improving Intentionality And Observance Of Time 131

Work-Life Balance And Stress Reduction 139

Knowing What Productivity Is

Isn't being productive a small obsession for all of us? The notion of productivity is not new. The idea has been around for a while and is still being discussed, particularly in business, where the goal is to increase the efficiency of labor in order to increase profits.

In order to maximize our time, avoid wasting energy, and, ultimately, produce the greatest profits or better outcomes; humans are constantly developing and improving productivity, whether it is in the business, economic, or personal spheres.

Nowadays, being productive is more of a personal goal in the world. We do not have infinite access to information, particularly now that the majority of us are connected via technology and the internet. Although accessibility has increased, procrastination and an abundance of information have also resulted.

Because there are so many distractions around us, the digital age is also the most unproductive period of human history. When this occurs, we look for productivity tricks via books, apps, blogs, and other resources even more.

This book was written to assist you in separating business from personal life and to assist us in setting our own filters and boundaries since we believe that this is a vital endeavor. But first, it's important to define productivity. In addition to the personal definition, there is the corporate definition.

The Definition of Business

Given that we are currently discussing productivity, it would be beneficial to familiarise ourselves with its business application. Productivity is often discussed in terms of financial performance in business. Productivity, in the words of Thanh Pham of Asian Efficiency, is the result you obtain for each input you provide. For instance, you might anticipate receiving one liter of orange juice if you give five oranges. However, if someone else can extract one liter of orange juice from four oranges, then, just by using fewer oranges to produce the same amount of juice, this person is more productive than you.

Increasing productivity entails either decreasing input relative to output or increasing output relative to input. This explains why phrases like "cutting down expenses" and "increasing our profit margin" are used in business.

The Individual Defined

When discussing productivity on a personal level, the first thing we should consider is how arbitrary or variable it is. Personal productivity is defined in an arbitrary way. Chris Bailey claims in "A Life of Productivity" that each person's level of productivity varies.

A banker might define productivity as directing a team of 100 workers and achieving high sales, while a recent graduate might define productivity as retiring at age 30 and living a modest life thereafter. While an engineer may define productivity as completing daily activities within a tight time frame, a basketball coach can define productivity as crossing everything off their to-do lists. Productivity to a fatigued parent can mean getting their youngster to bed by 8 o'clock.

Being productive in the tasks we perform is the ultimate goal for many of us who strive for increased personal productivity. In the end, we want to accomplish more in less time by being more proficient at what we do. It also involves learning how to manage the different types of information and accessibility while maintaining our attention on the current task at hand, all without delaying our progress on ongoing projects.

The Resources Needed to Reach Efficiency

Our productivity can be achieved with very basic tools. They are: ● Our unique systems ● Our capacities as individuals ● Our actions

● Our options, needs, and demands

Every aspect of our lives, including our interests, finances, relationships, parenting, and housework, can benefit from increased personal productivity.

Your Values

This book will attempt to start you out on a road toward being productive by concentrating on your thoughts, your space as well and your emotions. However, ultimately, you determine your own productivity by building up your own practice based on what you've gained in this book.

This book is a tool to help you reorganize your priorities and discover the numerous ways in which you can reinvent your everyday routines, so do not be scared to change these approaches and the concepts in this book. You want it to meet your priorities, and it always comes back to the value you place on your systems, your duties and your values.

None of us are static; life evolves based on the priorities we have and the ideals we set. Productivity as a practice can change with our values as we continue growing.

What Evernote Can Do For You

Evernote has shown to be a useful tool that lets users store and retrieve data from any location at any time. In other words, anyone can keep working on certain files without carrying around other devices. Thanks to this program, you may now travel and continue working on projects without needing to bring along a laptop, phone, tablet, or another comparable device. Simply save a file (a text, document, picture, etc.) into Evernote, then retrieve it later to carry out additional editing, share it with other users, or accomplish nearly any other task. Beyond just being a place to store notes, Evernote is so much more than that.

To get the most out of Evernote, learn about its features and give it a try. The main purpose of this software is note storage. Almost every file and remark the user has can be stored there. Evernote supports bookmarks, photos, web pages, and any type of written document. The notes can be retrieved at a later time, thanks to their indexing. Geolocation tags can even be added to notes to help with better and more precise filing. It is capable of more than that.

Clipper Web

The web clipper add-on for Evernote is largely unknown to users. Users typically use the browser's bookmark function to save online pages when they don't have Evernote. However, this will simply save the page and prevent you from taking notes on that specific article.

Using a simple bookmark would access a page later without indicating whether a portion of the page was previously useful or interesting. To access a saved page, one would need to peruse the page and quickly identify the crucial sections. Time-consuming if the page is dense with content, not to mention the plethora of advertisements, pictures, and other oddities that frequently appear on websites. Select portions of a webpage can be cut and stored with Evernote Web Clipper. This makes it easier for later use because the user can just store the sections that are useful. In addition, there is more organization and less clutter.

A whole page or certain sections of a page can be highlighted and stored in Evernote. These stored web pages can be annotated or notes made on. All of this is made possible with Evernote's web-clipping plugin.

Opera, Safari, and Google Chrome are the best browsers for using the Evernote Web Clipper feature. With a different installation, it might still function with other browsers, though. On the internet, users can quickly highlight, clip, and archive interesting content for later reading. In addition to web articles, Evernote users can take screenshots, bookmark websites, and clip emails and PDF documents. You may even save an entire pages.

Simply find the Clipper option on Evernote and utilize it. Choose an option, an additional note or a tag on the selected web section; by doing this, the selected clipping will be sent to

Evernotefor filing and storage. The note includes a stored copy of the web address. In this manner, the user can choose to return to the page at a later time. The note has the URL attached, so it won't take up space on the note itself. It's simple to bookmark and return to online pages, including recipes, crafts, research articles, and fascinating articles, at any time. Like other notes, the online clippings can also be tagged.

The web pages that you clipped can also be annotated. The Web Clipper comes with a number of markup tools that users can use. Web pages that have been marked up can then be saved for subsequent use or reference. It can also be distributed by email or social media. The ability to keep annotated or clipped web pages in the same way as regular notes is the greatest feature of

EvernoteWeb Clipper. It is just as easily categorized and arranged as standard typewritten notes. Once the Evernote account is opened, all saved web pages and web page clips are readily available for reading and searching at any time. Users are no longer required to return to the website.

Google can also be integrated with the web clipper. That is, relevant site clippings saved on Evernote show up on the right side of the search results screen the next time a user uses Google's search options to look up a particular topic. In this manner, the user receives a reminder or can view the web pages they have already viewed. Since the pages have previously been perused, it is simpler to go back to them or to determine which ones to skip. Open Evernote's settings button and click the

"Related Results" box to enable this feature.

Large-Scale Note Management

Retrieving a large number of files and notes from a PC, laptop, or external device can be very annoying. To find specific notes, one had to go through a lengthy list of files. The majority of gadgets lack convenient and dependable filtering tools. Evernote is incredibly good at organizing a lot of notes. Its note-archiving and note-filtering system is incredible. Notes that have been stored can be arranged in notebooks to facilitate quick retrieval. Additionally, Evernote features a tagging system that expedites and simplifies note search and retrieval. To improve and expedite searching even further, hyperlinks can be noted.

Consider this: for a single, large office project, a person on a home computer stores roughly 20 files. These files contain a variety of formats, including text documents, lists, media material, and web connections. Then there's the one big file that has all the information combined into a single presentation. To obtain a few informational snippets, each person working on the project would have to scroll through all 20 of these files. Twenty files can be too many to manage. Imagine being required to go through thousands of them now.

Organizing a tonne of notes is made easier using Evernote. It facilitates retrieval as well. Even notes can be automatically archived into specific notebooks to meet filing organization needs more quickly and easily.

Take Note of the Links

Another Evernote tool that makes archiving and accessing multiple notes easier is note linkages. When notes start to accumulate, this is quite beneficial. Users would not have to navigate through multiple notes in search of relevant information by connecting them together.

Right-click the note you want to link in order to establish a note link. Choose "Copy Note Link." Copy the link and paste it into another note so that it will link to the selected note. This will connect the two notes. Consequently, the other note would also appear automatically when one was searched for.

When writing an article, for example, you can put all of your related web research into one note, the article into another, and the outline into still another. In this manner, the overview note and research note will also appear when the article is opened or searched for. This eliminates the need to search separately for the other two notes and to open several notebooks to find them.

Additionally, users can expedite the opening of recently or often viewed notes from Evernote. A quick access button will show up in Evernote when you drag the note to the toolbar. Then, frequently used notes will only need to be clicked.

Time Management Is A Requirement Of Leadership.

A proficient time manager is also regarded as a superior leader. Why is that? Because they take the necessary actions to achieve their company's objectives. They show up, investigate, identify areas and things that need to be adjusted, and use principles to make them function.

An effective time manager also understands how to inspire and guide others to find creative methods to make better use of their time. They set an exemplary example and freely share their knowledge and support.

As leaders, they constantly exchange strategies, ideas, and tactics for improving their time, situations, and state of affairs management.

Headship

Being an Internet business owner requires the entrepreneur to be a skilled time manager who can handle multiple tasks or enterprises at once and manage them all effectively.

If a net entrepreneur is losing clients, running out of time and unable to bill them for that, or unable to complete projects, they cannot have any success in their firm.

One of the most important markers of a home business enterpriser who effectively manages their time is their ability to handle projects. Do they govern by intention or by crises? Is reaching a desired outcome in project management a component of their plan to go either slowly or quickly?

This could have a negative impact on work-from-home entrepreneurs' chances of success in business and damage their online reputation. All of this is frequently connected to appropriate and successful time management! Is there a way around this obstacle?

Time = Management

Effective time management is undoubtedly the main objective of almost any work-from-home business seeking success. Their online enterprises suffer greatly when they are unable to manage their time effectively.

The majority of people who work from home and want to succeed in their ventures want to make creative use of their time. Efficient time management enables remote business owners to accomplish more in less time, satisfy customers, and maintain a stable business.

A specific set of abilities, tactics, and resources are needed for effective time management, which enables online business owners to use them to complete specific jobs, projects, and objectives. Without making smart use of their time, they are essentially wasting it and are unable to meet important corporate objectives.

For many reasons, online entrepreneurs find it extremely important to manage their time well in their home-based businesses.

They are capable of finishing tasks on schedule.

If they're prepared to finish projects efficiently, they'll handle more work, hire more staff, and better serve their clientele by effectively meeting deadlines.

They're more equipped to produce excellent work.

Work that is completed more slowly and with greater attention to detail is of higher quality. The only thing that can produce quality work is meticulous attention to detail and careful caring.

When they can fulfill deadlines, they will be able to get more work. As a piece receiving enterpriser, fulfilling deadlines for clients is a given! On the internet, almost everything is time. Sensitive in the sense that meeting deadlines demonstrates your responsibility and dedication to the work at hand.

R.O.I.

When an entrepreneur manages their time well, there is a significant return on investment when they pay close attention to details in their home business. They take less time to get the work done if they become more exhausted over time, yet they are still willing to make a comparable amount of money, if not less. They got a great return on their investment—planning time.

Decide on the Best Action

Once your priorities and strategy for achieving your primary objective have been set, Referring back to the earlier example, how can you study so that you can make the most of your time and knowledge acquisition after establishing your short-term objectives, such as studying diligently and applying what you have learned? For instance, if your short-term objective is to study diligently, you can come up with three strategies.

You start by reading your books over and over again. Second, you listen to your professor during class and read your books at home. Thirdly, you use supplemental tools to enhance your learning, such as instructional films and images, while also reading your books and paying attention to your professor. Which of these three approaches do you believe to be the most successful? The best way to improve retention when learning something is to use as many senses as possible, as method number 3 best illustrates. This also applies to every other sub-goal you have. To get the best outcomes, pick the one that functions the best.

Proceed!

A man who owed a lot of money previously lived. He owed money to everyone and everything. He owed money on a few other accounts: $50 from the neighborhood bakery, $100 from his neighbor, $5000 from his school loan, and $10,000 from the car he purchased last month. He made a self-promised effort to pay off all of his debts as soon as he secured employment. That's what he carried out. He settled his obligation from the bakery with his first pay period. He settled his debt with his neighbor with his second paycheck. He paid off his student loan from his third income to his twenty-fifth. He was also growing weary of working nonstop without being able to save anything for himself by the time he received his 26th paycheck.

He was growing dissatisfied. Even though he was starting to feel depressed, he kept up his loan payments. He was almost finished repaying his $10,000 debt when he made a mistake that cost him his job. With nothing left over to sustain himself, he used every last penny to pay off his debt. He was unable to take pleasure in his earnings and preserve any money for an emergency. He was at a loss for what to do and felt compelled to hold himself responsible for the current state of affairs.

Getting back on track is the second time management strategy that you must apply. Time management requires action, and you won't be able to complete it in the future if you don't do it now. As the saying goes, "It's now or never." Some people constantly persuade themselves that after doing this and that, they will do this and that. While it is true that you must complete one task at a time, remember to prioritize your needs over all other considerations. He prioritized paying off his obligations over saving money for himself, just like the man who was deeply in debt.

How did it affect him? Although he was able to settle his bills, he was left penniless and without anything to eat. Don't postpone your dreams if you wish to manage your time. Take immediate action on them. There would be no future for them, no time left. Keep in mind that chances only present themselves once in a lifetime, and in order to seize them, you must be able to recognize them.

Maintain a Work-Fun Balance

"Man dullness results from all work and no play." Though it seems so corny, this is the case. You won't benefit from working too much since, if you don't take occasional breaks from work, stress will eat you alive. Make time for yourself and take a break from your work. Take a break when you notice in the mirror that your eye bags are almost reaching your jaw, your stiffened hair is practically coming out of its roots, or your spectacles are already skewed.

These are indicators that your body needs to rest and that you are becoming overly worked up. Adjust your spectacles, brush your hair, and place a cucumber slice over each eye. In order to revitalize yourself and divert your attention from work, take a nap; finding the right balance between work and play doesn't always require you to travel or attend parties; it can also mean that you need to enjoy what you are doing. You would probably enjoy it if you were passionate about what you did. If your work is fulfilling, it will soon turn into a simple pleasure for you. Furthermore, doing your responsibilities won't be as difficult as they were previously if it turns into a pastime.

Acquiring and Applying Fundamental Time Management Skills to Achieve Success in College

Based on my observations from teaching college for many years and the comments from hundreds of students, time management is the biggest obstacle to college success.

Definition of time management

The ability to plan your day and evening such that you accomplish your tasks and yet have time for enjoyment is known as time management. That's how I define it, at least! It indicates that you are in charge of your time and that time is neither running away from you nor controlling you in such a way that you conclude the day wondering where the time went and are unable to identify the tasks you set out to complete.

Why College Time Is Unique

You won't encounter what I've learned to be the particular time constraints associated with college known as "college time," or C-Time, until your special college years, unless you end up a college lecturer like me. C-Time is a special, intense period of time, unlike anything you have ever experienced in your prior school years. You get a week off for Christmas, another week off in the spring, and two months off over the summer, but college offers you even more time off in addition to more concentrated academic time.

You begin either in early September or at the end of August. If you are an American student, you often have four days of classes without any significant breaks until Thanksgiving. After that, you will graduate early in December and have a lengthy four- to six-week break from school in January. Restarting in late

January or early February, you complete the course in late April or early May, and you may then take the entire months of June, July, and August off.

While the average American worker receives only a few weeks of vacation, college students typically receive four months off annually!

Is there another employment that offers you that much time off?

The months that you spend in school are extremely demanding, which is a drawback. They give you so much time off because of this! to get better!

You must be prepared for the rigorous pace of the Fall and Spring semesters if you wish to succeed in college. This is not to say that you don't pace yourself. To prevent burnout, you need to pace yourself. However, you still need to be conscious of the fact that you are pacing yourself in a highly time-sensitive setting.

You will perform far better in college if you embrace that as a given than if you try to customize requirements and deadlines to fit your schedule. This will not only result in a lot of irate lecturers having to explain to you why you are not able to reschedule your examinations or turn in your term paper one week later without getting in trouble. However, it makes it more probable that you won't receive the A grade that you presumably want.

Here's another significant way that C-Time differs from the majority of previous experiences you will have in life with regard to time management. We discuss how important it is to focus on one task at a time. Right now, all I have on my mind is finishing this book. August is here, and I'm off from teaching this month. It is expected of you as a student and of me as a professor to juggle five separate courses. Five classes! To achieve the best grade possible in each of those courses, you must devote your full attention to them all. You have to focus on your fifth course, philosophy, or that music choice that turned out to be harder than you anticipated, even though yourfavorite subject to study is astronomy, your obligatory science course.

If you find that five classes a semester is too much for you, you can always take four and make up the fifth course during the summer or during winter break, as this book has mentioned on prior occasions. The drawback of doing that is that you lose out on taking advantage of those four months, which are such a gift for college students, to do other exciting things like traveling, working a part-time or full-time job for experience or money, or doing an internship for credit. These are things that may be much more difficult to accomplish after graduation and after you land a traditional full-time 9–5 job.

The good news is that your chances of managing all the expectations placed on you in a given semester will rise if you acquire fundamental time management skills. This is due to the fact that learning to prioritise is the most important time management concept, especially for college students. Setting priorities includes deciding what is essential to learn and study for each course, completing it, and planning your daily schedule for the semester to ensure that you finish what has to be done. It also involves saying "no" to things that are not important.

Setting goals is behind prioritizing. You're more likely to be able to prioritize and attain the successful outcomes you need to finish each semester of college and graduate if you have both short- and long-term goals.

Establishing goals

We fail without goals, which is why they are important. However, objectives must be precise rather than broad. One may aspire to graduate from college. However, how about a more focused objective? I would like to earn a college degree that is as near to a 4.0 as feasible.

My goal is to earn a degree in a subject for which I have a genuine passion after college.

Having taken full use of my winter and summer breaks, my goal is to graduate from college in four years.

Both immediate and long-term objectives

Establishing both short-term and long-term goals is part of time management. Everything from this hour, this day, this week, or this month is a short-term aim.

The long view is represented by long-term goals. When you imagine yourself in twenty years, that is, by the end of this year, by the end of college, by the end of five years, etc.

These objectives are not set in stone. But having them is beneficial. It keeps you inspired and on course.

Thus, give your short-term objectives considerable thought.

Consider the following questions, then record your responses in writing. I plan to accomplish this before the end of this month.

By the end of this week, I will have completed this.

I'm going to finish this by the end of today.

In one hour, I will have finished this assignment.

Apply the same logic to your long-term objectives.

I want to have achieved this by the end of the year.

This goal is part of my two-year strategy.

I will have achieved this goal in five years.

I envision myself accomplishing this goal in ten years.

Making Plans

Whether you're taking fully online courses, hybrid courses that combine online and in-person learning, or in-person lectures, scheduling is the key to effective time management, especially for college students.

The Value Of Having An Ordered Work Area

We discussed how important it is to set up your "head space" for the goals you have for your business in the last section.

This brings us to our next essential core element for effective time management and productivity: creating a physically comfortable and well-suited work environment.

Using effective productivity techniques is quite challenging when your home office is messy and disorganized. Many people find that a messy workspace and desk translate into a congested head, which is something we do not want.

On the other hand, there seems to be something about a well-ordered workspace that instantly places one in the frame of mind necessary for productivity and clarity on the tasks at hand.

I think that this part will help you establish a welcoming and productive work environment that will serve as the model for your new and enhanced productive work zone!

Step Three

After that, you ought to spend money on a reliable storage solution. It can be easier to search for pre-built workplace storage systems to do this. You won't have to try to picture what you might need in this way. A number of designers have produced home office storage cabinets in response to the surge in work-from-home entrepreneurs. There are several sizes of home offices available, ranging from little workspaces to expansive workspaces. IKEA is one of my favorite stores for excellent storage at affordable costs. Even if you're not a fan of IKEA, just perusing some of the room displays can inspire you with some fantastic ideas. What they can accomplish in some of the smallest places is astounding.

Having photos of your loved ones all about you is a smart idea. Don't overdo it if you plan to meet with clients in your home office. Adding encouraging words and photographs to place on the wall is also a terrific idea. Whatever keeps you focused on your task without detracting from it is acceptable and ideal.

Selecting the Most Important Work Tools

These days, with digital management tools becoming more and more important for businesses, we live in an incredible time. Never before has it been so simple to stay connected across several devices and be ready to quickly take your work on the go.

What do you currently own and use, and how much do you intend to work from home?

primary computer

This will be a desktop or laptop computer for a lot of individuals. You will undoubtedly need some sort of home computer setup if you plan to establish an office at home and run any demanding programs. This seems perfect for companies that use photography and graphic design services. If you were to use simply your laptop, you most likely wouldn't get the screen size you require. On the other hand, if your primary computer is a laptop, setting up extra monitors is rather simple.

A laptop computer is likely to be the most practical choice for you if your firm is more mobile in nature. Having a desktop and laptop computer is a common decision made by individuals who work from home most of the time. This allows them to work from anywhere at any time.

iPads and Tablet Computers

These portable gadgets have grown in popularity recently. Although it's doubtful that you could operate your company for extended amounts of time on an iPad or tablet, these devices are ideal for work that needs to be done on the go for some kinds of businesses. With the iPad, you may effortlessly perform business calls, check your email, conduct research, and even write your newest novel. This is more of a luxury item, in my opinion, than anything someone would pick over a laptop.

Smartphones The manner in which a lot of individuals conduct business these days has been altered by smartphones. With a smartphone, you can be linked virtually anywhere in the world. (Note that when traveling abroad, there are other expenses or factors to take into account, but in many cases, this is relatively simple.) In addition to having your phone line for calls and texts, you can do almost anything with your smartphone that you could do with an iPad or tablet.

Time Management Instruments Required

Numerous products on the market make the promise to help you become a better time manager. Every day, more and more accessories are added. I was able to find over 136 million results when I searched for "Time Management Tools" on Google, making it difficult to compare the various tools. In fact, it would be very easy to get drawn into the maelstrom of finding solutions to increase your productivity, only to realize that you have wasted so much time on the hunt that you could have begun your path to improved management techniques instead.

When it comes to time management tools, I have a simple guideline that applies to all devices. A tool helps you practice a skill more effectively rather than teaching you a new one. For example, you cannot learn to use Microsoft® Outlook 365 or any similar program to improve your communication skills. Nonetheless, you can improve your ability to send and receive messages. Similarly, while using a calculator can make you faster and more accurate in maths, it does not teach you how to compute.

In the same vein, you cannot learn time management skills from a tool. Reminders, applications, and calendars help streamline and expedite the organizing process. However, in order to make the best use of them, you will need to learn how to become more efficient in managing your time. That's when a tool can assist you in increasing your effectiveness. I would recommend the following to you: After you have mastered the time management techniques in this book and implemented them into your daily job, select an application that will increase your accuracy and efficiency.

In my humble view, all you need to explore time management approaches is a basic tool that can perform the following four functions:

Enables time schedule on a calendar

A digital calendar is among the most helpful tools that are out there. You can mark your workdays each week and set aside time each day for working and non-working activities on any calendar. Setting start and end timings for projects, allocating time to perform obligations, and scheduling meetings with others as needed are all excellent organizational habits. You might let others access your itinerary so they can schedule time with you. Alternatively, you might delegate the calendaring tasks to an administrative assistant.

One topic I get asked a lot is whether people should use different agendas or just one calendar, such as keeping separate schedules for work and personal purposes. If someone works more than one job, some of them may even have several professional goals. I know people who maintain many calendars and review their daily schedules utilizing the combined view. To manage who can view which calendar, security is the most frequent reason why individuals wish to utilise several calendars. Then, different groups of people can see different tasks. For instance, my family members don't need to view my work schedule; they can view my personal calendar. In a similar vein, my coworkers can see my work calendar but not my personal calendar. Those who play several roles or jobs can benefit from having different calendars. It is feasible to grant one group of people access to one calendar and another group of people access to another in order to make scheduling easier.

Although it is technically possible to use multiple calendars with any scheduling application, I do not advise doing so if you already struggle with time management. Several calendars will complicate time management, even when you use a consolidated view for yourself. I suggest creating a single calendar to record all of your obligations, both personal and professional. Simple techniques for delineating duties are available in digital calendars, such as the ability to mark particular events with color. Every member of the family may have a designated color on a calendar. To add your work schedule, just add new categories with different colors. For example, you may have one color for meetings, another for recurrent chores at work, and a separate color for personal time. If you see that using numerous calendars is actually necessary when you get proficient at time management, you can switch to doing so.

Meanwhile, you can provide several groups of individuals with varying degrees of calendar visibility, as indicated below:

Complete View

Individuals at this level get access to your whole calendar, which includes all of the meeting information, every meeting, and the times that you are available or occupied. By looking at the meeting's name and the information on the calendar invite, they may tell what you are doing. Giving someone this kind of access is uncommon and frequently unneeded. You might need to grant this degree of visibility in specific circumstances, such as when working with a close colleague whose job depends on yours and vice versa.

Author availability

This gives someone the capacity to add, remove, or modify meetings and tasks from your calendar. Your administrative assistant, for instance, might be listed as an author on your calendar. It is still possible to set up private meetings that are inaccessible to the calendar creator.

Free/heavy usage

This level displays the hours that are available and occupied, but it hides the specifics of each commitment. This is the most typical access level that is offered for a calendar. In actuality, this degree of exposure is offered by default to everyone in the majority of calendaring programs that I have used.

Absence of visibility

The calendar cannot be viewed as a result. A lot of CEOs won't give anyone access to their schedule. Making an appointment with them can only be arranged by getting in touch with them personally or through their administrative assistant.

One other feature of calendaring systems is the ability to make some tasks and meetings private. No one else, not even those with author or full access, will be able to view assignments or meetings that are marked private. Of course, if you'd like, you can let your "author" see these private tasks and meetings. Individuals with limited calendar access will be unable to view information and will have the time marked as "busy."

Sort meetings in the calendar by color.

On your calendar, use color to indicate time based on parameters that you define and can later adjust as needed. Adding color coding to your calendar entries to highlight events can give them more significance and improve the organization by classifying the entries.

You can decide quickly which chores are required and which may be easily rescheduled if needed by color-coding tasks and meetings. This tagging technique also makes it easier to analyze and reflect on a period of time so that changes can be made for future use. Keep in mind that the majority of solutions that allow you to color-code meetings also include a grayscale for those who are colorblind.

Make Sure You Have A Proper Daily Strategy Before You Begin Each Morning.

I trained to be a single-engine airplane pilot many years ago. My flying instructor, Nick, stressed the value of performing some pre-flight inspections before takeoff during our first lesson. A visual walk-around to examine the plane's movable parts was one of these checks, along with examinations of the fuel lines, tire pressure, engine and oil levels. After ensuring everything was functioning properly from the outside, Nick gave me the go-ahead to enter the cabin and perform many checks on the instruments and cockpit.

Since my earliest flying experiences, I have recognized that pre-flight and pre-landing inspections are crucial for every takeoff and landing, regardless of the aircraft size—from a tiny, single-engine plane to a big jumbo jet. I bring this up because part of effectively controlling your sales area involves doing a number of "pre-flight checks" each morning; I refer to this process as generating a daily territory plan!

The main reason most salespeople find it difficult to manage their time and territory as well as they might is, I would have to say, a lack of preparation every month, every week, and then every weekday morning.

Organized account managers will be more productive if they take the time to write up a plan for the day before they start working.

Taking into account all the responsibilities a territory manager has at the start of the workday, organizing the next day is the most crucial daily activity. This is so that, before your "journey" even starts, you may properly plan how you're going to handle any hectic day through weekly, monthly, and daily preparation.

The adage, "People don't plan to fail, they fail to plan," is undoubtedly familiar to you. It is inconceivable for a professional territory manager to begin their day without a written plan outlining their destination and the tasks they need to complete, just as it is unthinkable (as well as unsafe and unprofessional) for a pilot to fly from one airport to another without first completing those pre-flight checks prior to takeoff.

The daily territorial planning procedure comprises five steps

While creating a yearly, monthly, and weekly sales plan is important, for the time being, I only want to concentrate on assisting you in creating a daily plan. The five steps below will help you prepare your day in the morning before you go out into your sales area on workdays. This will help you feel more focused and productive throughout the day.

By setting aside time to develop a daily plan, you'll also feel more in charge of your life going forward, particularly when things don't go as planned and you're under pressure.

Examine your sales and territory targets for the upcoming week and month.

As part of your daily routine, the first thing you should do is go over and confirm your weekly and monthly territory goals, sales targets, and any other KPIs that you need to reach for the month. What are some of the company's objectives or activities that you should be focusing on this week and today?

Before today's business shuts, are there any tenders, quotations, or proposals that you need to finish or send out? Do you have any specific campaigns, promotions, or offers that you would like to share with your consumers during your sales appointments today? If yes, did you set aside time on your calendar for these chores today?

Are you confident that you'll reach your monthly sales target based on your current month's sales performance?

2. Go over yesterday's review

Examining your diary, calendar, spiral notebook, and inbox for the previous day's entries, emails, and notes is the second phase in the daily planning process. Review your calendar of events and the notes you wrote in your spiral notebook during the sales calls, and make sure you have sent out all of the emails. Look for any commitments you made to clients, remember all of the follow-ups and any requests, assignments, or tasks from yesterday that need to be completed today.

Move any tasks that are still unfinished from yesterday's lists to today's list so you can finish them today.

Additionally, see if there is anything you need to follow up on that you noted in your notebook from the phone calls, talks, or sales meetings you had yesterday. You see, it's crucial to have a plan to assist close all of the "loops" that remain open from yesterday's events before you can begin to consider what you must accomplish today.

3. Tomorrow's preview

The third phase is to check ahead on your calendar and take a quick glance at the events and appointments you have scheduled for the following few days.

Yes, you should plan ahead and consider what will happen in your sales territory over the next several days before you start concentrating on what you'll do today.

Do you have any scheduled sales meetings, for instance, that you might need to reschedule, reschedule, or reschedule? Do you have any impending deadlines that you need to meet in order to finish a sales pitch, customer purchase, credit, or return an item? Are there any reports, project milestones, or other tasks that you need to finish later this week? If so, will you have enough time today to begin or finish these tasks? Additionally, have you scheduled time in your calendar for today or later this week to work on these tasks? Over the next three days, when you review your calendar, ask yourself the following questions:

Which clients and potential clients am I planning to see later this week?

For these next customer visits, do I have the appropriate brochures, samples, collateral, or documents?

Should I pick them up from my sales office if I'm not ready to go, or may I view them online before coming to these appointments?

Personally, as you look over your schedule, see if there are any events in your personal life that take place after work hours. What personal follow-ups or tasks do you need to remember to complete or attend to?

By looking ahead to any upcoming personal obligations, you can reduce the likelihood of becoming anxious about things you've scheduled for later in the week that don't include work.

Being aware of your schedule for the rest of the week aids in maintaining control over your time today. Knowing that you're on top of all forthcoming meetings, territorial events, and personal responsibilities makes you feel good.

Disruptions

Those pop-up alerts telling you there's a new email in your inbox or a message from Facebook Messenger can be really distracting when you're working hard at your computer. Pop-up alerts encourage multitasking, which is something you should avoid doing when you have important tasks that must be finished by a certain date.

Interruptions are inevitable and unforeseen in the midst of other obligations and deadlines relating to the workplace. Sometimes, it begins out harmlessly enough, but as it keeps happening throughout the day, it gets more and more frequent, leaving you feeling disoriented, overburdened, and even angry. Interruptions frequently have the consequence of producing intense tension.

Even though we'd like to think we can multitask and adapt to the demands of the day, interruptions can accumulate and reduce productivity if you let them. It shifts your attention from the current task to another task or circumstance. It may result in overwhelming, inefficient, and unproductive labor for you. Even your job satisfaction may be impacted.

Interruptions have a direct way of taking our valuable time, whether they take the shape of an urgent meeting, unforeseen personal obligations, emails, or pointless talks with coworkers. As this occurs every day, it irritates us more and depresses us, especially when there is significant work that needs to be done.

While some disruptions are avoidable, many are not. It is your duty to develop the ability to distinguish between required and unnecessary disruptions. An option for those interruptions that are unavoidable is to learn how to better handle this.

As you work on your computer, be sure that your current status indicates that you are offline or busy in order to handle messenger interruptions. By doing this, you won't be sidetracked by pointless messages. You can include a professional yet friendly personal remark, such as "I will respond later," if you set your current status to "busy." This will let the person attempting to get in touch know that while you find their message essential, you are currently unavailable and will answer at a later time.

If you determine that the issue is urgent, you can choose to address it immediately or prioritize completing a portion of your current task. Many requests can wait until a later time, even if they might appear urgent to the sender. This thus offers you the authority to decide when to attend to the person's needs. For instance, you may put the assignment on your calendar for the following day or arrange a meeting with this person. Here's where setting priorities comes in handy.

By taking this strategy, you avoid being stressed out or feeling overburdened and manage your responsibilities. In addition to respecting the other person's request, you are also being considerate of your own time. It is not necessary to contend with disruptions. Acquire the skill to properly handle them while maintaining consideration for the needs of others.

You never know what distractions the day will bring until you start working on your daily priorities. That means that a portion of you needs to be adaptable to your timetable. You might receive a crucial email or call that requires quick attention. This demonstrates flexibility.

Avoid letting the anticipation of distractions cause you to lose concentration on the task at hand. You won't be able to properly unwind and concentrate on your crucial assignment as a result. Yes, interruptions do actually make it difficult to concentrate, but keep in mind that you can manage some interruptions while being powerless over others. It might be frustrating because losing focus does mean losing your creative output. Getting into a "reactive mode" is what you want to avoid doing. Set priorities, concentrate on the tasks at hand, and accept interruptions according to their significance.

Orient Yourself To Succeed

You cannot be disorganized or have any ongoing obligations if you want to prosper financially. I sincerely hope that my readers will be able to handle their own financial situations on their own. As a result, this chapter will assist readers in taking care of their own financial organization and debt management.

Taking Care of Debt: Debt is a cruel thing. You are probably not haunted by debt if you make all of your required payments on time. Nonetheless, you should adhere to the advice in this section for handling debt if you are falling behind on your payments or finding it difficult to make them.

Setting priorities is essential to debt management. Generally speaking, you should pay off the debt that is costing you the most in interest and fees first. If you have two credit cards with equal balances but different interest rates, for instance, figure out which one is costing you more. It makes sense to prioritize paying off card 1 first and only making the minimum payment on card 2, as card 1 has a twenty percent interest rate while card 2 has a ten percent interest rate. Experts maintain that making lump sum payments on only one credit card at a time is the most efficient approach to paying off several credit cards. Furthermore, never forget to make your minimum monthly payment—missing one might have terrible consequences for your finances.

Alternatively, paying off the lowest credit card debt before focusing on the larger accounts might have psychological benefits. Millionaire David Ramsey, who was once bankrupt, claims that he was motivated to pay off any obligation, no matter how tiny. He advises people who are feeling extremely overwhelmed by their bills to begin their path to financial security by paying off any outstanding, manageable loans first. Even though there are more obligations overall—even though the total amount owed is higher than if one major bill had been prioritized—the other debts will appear more manageable because there are fewer of them overall. You will have to weigh the higher interest costs against the psychological advantage of paying off a loan promptly.

Certain past-due accounts are also sent to a collections agency. An organization has the right to forward an account to an independent organization that will retrieve the money on its behalf if they are not paid in a timely way. Put differently, you may end up in conflict with a collections agency if you don't pay your payments on time. Regretfully, your credit score will suffer if you don't pay the collections agency within the allotted time, which is often sixty days. Therefore, in the long run, it will be beneficial to pay off your accounts that are not under the control of a collections agency before you make significant payments toward those that have gone to collections, even if you have some accounts in collections and others that are in good standing. This will stop new debts from adding to the ones that already have an impact on your credit score.

A settlement represents an additional choice for managing debt. You may be able to reach an agreement with the credit card company to pay your outstanding balance for less than what was originally due. While some businesses are content to accept a part of the debt and forgive the remainder in order to avoid wasting resources pursuing payment for what you owe them, not all businesses will be amenable to a settlement. Ask to talk with a representative who is qualified to negotiate a debt settlement when you call your credit card company. If you are willing to construct a very short-term payment plan or make a lump sum payment, that will be beneficial to your case. However, be aware that as part of the settlement, the credit card company can want to restrict your credit limit or cancel your card.

If you are currently dealing with multiple high-interest bills, you might want to think about applying for a debt consolidation loan. For instance, a person may be in debt from numerous credit cards, medical bills, and utility payments. Loans for debt consolidation are designed for people who owe money to many institutions.

In accordance with the conditions of this arrangement, a wealthy creditor consents to settle the debtor's remaining amounts, sparing the debtor money on interest that would otherwise accrue. In return, the debtor makes consistent monthly payments to the creditor until the entire debt, including the interest charged by the creditor, is settled. Less than what the debtor would have paid the original creditors for their loans, the creditor obtains interest from the debtor.

Well-intentioned people list several advantages of debt consolidation loans. Specifically, they avoid paying interest. Furthermore, a debt consolidation loan will typically result in fewer calls from collection agencies for the debtor. Additionally, as long as the debtors pay the creditor on time, their individual credit scores are maintained. A debt consolidation loan, one of several debt management strategies, functions by consolidating all of a person's outstanding debts into a single lump sum liability.

Bankruptcy is yet another option available to you for debt management. Despite what the general public believes, filing for bankruptcy won't release you from your outstanding bills.

Most Chapter 7 bankruptcy filings require the debtor to repay their creditors in fewer than six months. They are able to make their payments without using cash, nevertheless. The debtor may decide to sell or liquidate his or her valuables and assets under the terms of a Chapter 7 filing. The proceeds from the sale of such assets are then used to settle the debt owed to the creditors. Which belongings should be sold to make the debtor's asset loss reasonable for their circumstances will be decided by the courts.

You could be able to keep most or all of your estate in certain circumstances. Federal law exempts some goods from Chapter 7 bankruptcy. The kinds of assets that may be exempt from a Chapter 7 filing vary according to the state. You may be shocked to learn that, provided you meet your state's requirements, you can file for bankruptcy while keeping all of your belongings.

However, if you have a consistent source of income, you probably meet the requirements to file under Chapter 13. You might think about filing for Chapter 13 bankruptcy if you can show the court evidence of your income, such as a pay stub. In a Chapter 13 agreement, the debtor presents a detailed payment plan outlining their plan to pay off their outstanding obligations. The debtor will be granted Chapter 13 bankruptcy, which offers federal protection against additional debt collection harassment if the judge determines that the applicant can fulfill the requirements of their own proposal.

Discover Your Specialisation

The most important step in becoming an expert is identifying your specialization. You cannot become an expert if you have nothing to become an expert in. If you don't already know, a niche is a role or location that you are well-suited for and feel at ease in. There are numerous methods for identifying your niche, and I'll go over two here.

Five Steps

Finding your specialty is keeping you from reaching your full potential as a business expert, even while your goal is to become an expert in a particular industry. This can be quite difficult. Even though you've already taken the time to compile a list of all the things you're interested in and enthusiastic about, you still don't feel like you've found the proper field.

It can paralyze you mentally to put so much pressure on yourself to find your specialization. While identifying the ideal niche is crucial, there are instances when it's preferable to just get started. Once you get going, you can begin experimenting with your various concepts. This enables you to pick up new skills or approaches to your profession and learn from your failed company ventures.

The following five steps will assist you in identifying your niche:

Determine your interests and areas of enthusiasm.

Most likely, you've already completed this; in case not, jot down a list of ten things you are really passionate about. Your business will push you at some point. Your chances of quitting a business are higher if it is something you have no interest in.

That does not imply that you have to locate the ideal company. You will be more likely to stick with a job if you can ensure that you enjoy at least some aspects of it. You won't stick with it if there's nothing about it that you like.

These inquiries should point you in the correct path if you appear to be struggling to identify your interests:

When you have free time, what do you like to do? When nothing else is going on, what are the things you look forward to?

Which magazines do you enjoy reading? Which subjects are you most interested in learning about?

Do you belong to any groups or associations?

Determine the challenges you are capable of handling.

You can begin to reduce your options now that you have your list of ten. You need to identify your target market and their issues if you want to become an authority and build a sustainable business. Next, you must determine whether you are able to resolve their issues. The following techniques could be applied to determine potential issues within a niche:

Speak one-on-one with your target audience. To obtain the finest responses, figure out how to ask the correct questions.

Browse discussion boards. Examine forums tailored to your niche and take note of the topics being addressed. What inquiries are being made? What issues do they have?

Go through the terms. Examine keyword combinations on websites like Trends or Google AdWords. This will display some helpful popular search terms for you.

Examine the opposition.

One should not view competition negatively. This may indicate that you've identified a profitable niche. Make sure you see their websites in their entirety. Create a spreadsheet and record the many places you discover related to your niche.

Next, try to figure out how you may differentiate yourself from your rivals. Is it still possible to rank in searches?

Content of poor quality. If your competitors' content is of poor quality, it will be simple to outperform them.

Little transparency. You will stand out from your faceless competitors if you decide to personalize your service and your competition is primarily corporate.

Hardly little paid rivalry. You have a strong chance to stand out if the keywords you researched return a high volume of search traffic but little in the way of paid advertising and competition.

Determine the profitability of your niche.

You need to be getting rather close to determining what your niche will be. Though you might not have been able to settle on just one concept, you ought to have a few that you enjoy. You may now see how much money you might be able to make in your niche. An excellent place to start your search is ClickBank.

Start examining the best services in your industry. Nothing appears in your search results. This is not a good indication. This could indicate that there hasn't been any success in making money off of that specific area.

It's encouraging if you find a respectable number of services—not an excessive number. To help you decide how much to charge for your products, make a list of the various price points.

Additionally, you are not required to develop your own product. In addition to working on your ideas, you have the option to collaborate with website owners, advertisers, or artists in your industry to earn commissions.

Try out the ideas you have had.

All that's left to do is put your chosen niche to the test—you have an abundance of information at your disposal to assist you in making this decision. Making a pre-sale landing page is an easy method to test your idea. Then, use some promotion to get them there.

Do not give up if you do not receive any pre-sales. You still have the option to choose a strong niche. This can simply indicate that you chose the incorrect service or that your sales pitch was weak.

For sixty minutes

One method of determining your specialty has previously been discussed, but it may not be the best approach for you. Since every individual is unique, here's an additional method for identifying a niche.

List all of your abilities and skills in writing.

Since these responses are relevant to the questions that follow, please answer honestly. Recognize the distinction between your strengths and your areas of wishful thinking. Is mastering a skill you've always wanted to acquire realistic, or is it just a pipe dream? Put all criticism aside and concentrate just on your abilities—not on whether they will enable you to earn money.

Which of those skills do you most enjoy using?

If there's a conflict between your heart and intellect, you'll be out of balance. In this situation, everything will seem right in your heart, but everything will feel wrong in your brain, and vice versa.

Sort the items on your initial list according to your preferences: the things you enjoy doing the most and the least. Next, consider what decisions you can make to eliminate.

Are there any activities you enjoy doing that people need?

Congratulations, you have just one audience if one of them really sticks out. A little investigation will assist you in reducing the number of options. To determine whether or not you should pursue a specialty, look at the demographics on websites that provide them.

Which of the needs you have identified will individuals be willing to pay for?

The essential word is pay. Even while your parents might be ready to give you a few bucks for anything you manufacture, you won't benefit from that in the long run. There's a good probability that if one customer will pay for your product, then there probably will be more.

Make sure you are telling the truth. Even though you enjoy playing football with your pals, you'll have a difficult time winning if you weigh more than 145 pounds.

If you genuinely know yourself, answering these four questions shouldn't take more than an hour. It's acceptable if you take longer if you don't find that it takes longer. To avoid wasting time later, it is crucial to take your time today.

Setting Up Your Objectives

If you're always working on urgent assignments but never seem to finish the proper things, you need a method to figure out what your daily goals will be. Here's how to make sure everything gets done, preferably in the order that indicates which goals you are actually trying to achieve.

Use the guidelines below to ensure that you understand what has to be done:

List all of your to-do items.

Create a brief list with every item on your to-do list. Encompassing large endeavors, small tasks, urgent "must-do now" tasks, as well as the "should-dos" that will enable you to reach your long-term goals. Nothing is overlooked if all of the tasks are kept on a single master list. Regardless of where an assignment comes from—phone calls, seminars, emails, or your in-basket—make sure it gets included in the master to-do list.

Sort by value

Assess the importance of every mission. Does it have a due date? Will it aid in achieving your objectives? What will happen if you don't take immediate action? Never confuse importance with urgency. Sort the items that are "To Do Now" from those that are "To Do Later." Make a short list of the top 12 things you need to get done right now. Put them in priority order.

Carrying the paperwork for the top 12 Do Now jobs in a 100% Recycled Expanding Report with Double Capacity Pockets. Sort the content according to priority order: put the best quality in the first box, the second-best in the next bag, etc. To rapidly access the Expanding File, hold it on your screen.

Writing out your goals for the day will help you easily remember all you need to get done. Even if there are a lot of to-do lists, this is getting better every day. Start writing the file in the notepad with the most important items first, and then add the less important ones.

Include in your list of things to do

Put your to-do list somewhere you can still see it: on your seat, in your note section on your phone, in your pocket, in your diary, or on your schedule. You won't ever forget that you have something to do if you continue to view the list. Write a brief note describing your alarm in bullet points or use a format. To begin with, you may jot down the precise deadline for doing the task, the materials you need for the mission, or the name of the person you will be meeting (if that is the case). Documents are extremely important for individuals who tend to forget things easily.

Establish reasonable deadlines for this.

If your management has given you a deadline while you're working on something, establish your own deadline prior to the time frame they have given you. Decide on sensible ones instead. You don't want to rush things to finish sooner. One step at a time, and try not to put yourself in a position where you will be disappointed.

This also applies to the daily work. Man, don't wear yourself out. Instead of pushing yourself to do anything, you want to accept the consequences of completing subpar work.

It doesn't like going the whole day without sleeping. Take a nap when you're tired. A quick nap or a 10- to 15-

minute food break is perfectly acceptable. As a general rule, unwind for ten minutes for every hour of assistance.

Move the commotion forward.

In this current society, a lot of things will prevent us from performing our jobs. These cover a wide range of devices, including smartphones, laptops, appliances, the Internet (particularly Facebook and Twitter), and more. If you're going to squander your time and energy on these things, how are you supposed to finish your work?

Set aside the issues that are causing you distress. Instead of checking your mailbox constantly, schedule times during the day to do so or during job breaks. It would be much easier to do the task if you began to pay less attention to these problems.

Regularly reevaluate

Examine projects in the growing database according to your rating system. As soon as you can, click through and clear the straightforward items on the list. Work on difficult tasks over extended periods of time and try to complete them when you're at your most alert. Evaluate unforeseen events as they happen. Add them to the master list of things to do. Every day, review your master's to-do list, make a fresh shortlist of things to accomplish, and rearrange the order of the items in your expanding file.

List the assignments in order of significance when you turn them into a journal. Make sure your handwriting is readable, and rewrite your paper on another tab. Advice: Did you know that, on average, larger fonts will motivate you to work harder than smaller fonts to finish the task?

After you've completed writing your daily or weekly to-do list, try to determine which chores or tasks are the least important and whether you really should be doing them. If so, you may need to adjust your daily schedule; if not, you may be able to commit to the other activities with greater flexibility, or you may choose to take some time to unwind.

The Value Of Effective Time Management

Our productivity, efficiency, and quality of life are directly impacted by how we spend time, which is a finite and valuable resource.

It's critical to acknowledge that, despite having the same number of hours in a day, some people accomplish far more than others.

Their approaches to time management diverge.

Time management experts strike a balance between their obligations, fulfilling deadlines, accomplishing objectives, and still finding time for leisure and hobbies.

However, improper time management can have a number of detrimental effects.

Work-life balance deteriorates, stress escalates, feelings of being overwhelmed take control, and procrastination sets in.

In addition, ineffective time management can result in decreased output, lower-quality work, stagnation of significant initiatives, and missed opportunities.

Goals for the Book

The goal of this book is to give readers a strong foundation in time management as well as the techniques and resources they need to increase their effectiveness and output.

The primary goals consist of:

Give a thorough explanation of the time management concept: Describe time management, how it affects our day-to-day activities, and why it is so important for success and well-being.

Provide workable plans and tried-and-true methods: Give people a range of time-saving strategies, advice, and insights that they can implement right away in their daily lives.

This will cover a variety of topics, such as planning strategies, outage management, prioritization, and concentration approaches.

Examine typical problems and offer solutions: Deal with common time management roadblocks like procrastination, low motivation, and persistent interruptions.

Provide doable and efficient methods for overcoming these obstacles and maintaining concentration on the most crucial activities. Adjust time management to various situations: Acknowledge that time management is relevant in both personal and professional spheres.

Examine particular coping mechanisms for handling the stress and expectations of the workplace and striking a good balance between job, family, hobbies, and self-care.

Maintain the interest and motivation of readers: Give advice and recommendations to help keep people motivated as they work to become better time managers.

Promote self-control, habit, and tenacity as essential components to attain long-lasting outcomes.

By the time you finish reading this book, you will have gained knowledge and useful skills that will enable you to greatly enhance your time management, increasing your productivity and efficiency and enabling you to savour every moment.

Chapter Eleven

Monitoring Development and Making Modifications Chapter Twelve

Maintaining Long-Term Expertise in Time Management Chapter 5

The Basis of Successful Time Management

Planning, arranging, and judicious use of your time are essential skills for achieving your priorities and objectives.

Because it increases productivity and lowers stress, it is essential for both professional and personal success.

You may prioritize work, establish clear goals, and allot time according to the urgency and importance of each task with the help of effective time management. By doing this, you can guarantee that important assignments are finished on schedule, avoiding last-minute rushes and decreasing the possibility of mistakes.

A sense of achievement and boosted self-confidence may result from this.

Resource utilization can be optimized with the aid of time management.

You can reduce wasted effort on pointless chores and concentrate on activities that help you achieve your long-term objectives by devoting time to task 6 according to their significance. This enhances efficacy and efficiency in both personal and professional spheres.

By managing your time well, you may also preserve a positive work-life balance. Allocating time for work, play, family, and self-care helps you stay out of burnout and keep your general well-being.

It guarantees that you have time for activities that revitalize your body and mind and help you avoid over-committing.

Overcoming procrastination is one of time management's challenges. Recognizing and countering this inclination is a necessary part of effective time management, and methods like the Pomodoro Technique or SMART goal-setting are common tools for doing so.

Employers place great importance on time management in the workplace. People who are good at managing their time are frequently seen as trustworthy, productive, and able to handle challenging jobs.

It also helps with teamwork because cooperative tasks require efficient time management and deadline compliance.

Evaluating How Much Time You Spend Now

Knowing how you now spend your time is crucial before you can begin to manage it efficiently. Analyzing your routines and distinguishing between productive and non-productive activities are necessary steps in evaluating how you currently use your time. To assist you in evaluating your present time utilization, follow these steps:

1. Track Your Time: Observing how you spend your time for a week or two is the first step towards evaluating how you use your time. You can keep track of your activities and the amount of time you spend on them using a spreadsheet, paper and ink, or an app that tracks your time.

2. Classify Your Actions: After keeping track of your time, divide your actions into three groups: neutral, non-productive, and productive. Activities that support your objectives, development as a person, or general well-being are considered productive. Activities like watching TV or spending a lot of time on social media are examples of non-productive ones since they don't offer value or are bad for your objectives. Activities like sleeping and commuting that neither increase nor decrease productivity are considered neutral.

3. Examine Your Results: Once your activities have been categorized, examine your results to find trends and potential areas for development. Consider the following: • What are the things I spend the most time on?

- How much time do I dedicate to idle pursuits?

- What are my favorite productive activities to engage in?

- Which ineffective tasks may I cut back on or do away with?

4. Recognise Time Wasters: One of the most important steps in evaluating how you use your time is to identify time wasters. Activities that take up a lot of time yet don't advance your objectives or general well-being are called time wasters. Procrastination, binge-watching TV, using social media excessively, and focusing too much time on unimportant chores are a few examples of time wasters. You can create plans to cut down on or get rid of your time wasters once you've recognized them.

5. Establish Priorities and Goals: Lastly, create meaningful goals and priorities using the knowledge you have obtained from evaluating how you utilize your time. Determine which activities are most essential to you and which have the biggest impact on your objectives, personal development, or general well-being based on your analysis. Make a calendar that reflects your values and priorities by using this information to help you prioritize your time.

To sum up, the first step towards efficient time management is to evaluate how you currently use your time. You can obtain insights into your time utilization and create time management plans by recording your time, classifying your activities, evaluating the outcomes, identifying time wasters, and creating goals and priorities.

Chapter 1: 13 Tricks for Cleaning

For single mothers, cleaning tips are especially crucial since they can come in quite handy while managing multiple obligations. The demanding juggle of children, work, and housework frequently leaves single mothers with little time or energy for thorough cleaning regimens.

Cleaning hacks are easy, fast, and practical ways to keep your house tidy and orderly without putting in a lot of extra time. These time-saving tips can help single mothers manage taking care of their kids while maintaining a clean home, all while making the most of their limited free time.

And stress-free living environment. They range from easy tactics to tactical organizational strategies that make clutter management more manageable.

Acknowledge "Clean Enough."

Perfection is frequently an unattainable aim due to the realities of solitary parenting. It's important to find satisfaction in the idea of "clean enough" instead. With kids, maintaining a tidy home is a constant struggle that leaves little time for other activities. But as a single mother, you will learn that spending quality time with your kids is more important than constantly trying to have swept carpets and dust-free corners.

It's quite reasonable to want a tidy, well-organized home. But you have to acknowledge that sometimes your situation might not allow you to attain flawless perfection. Accepting "clean enough" entails lowering standards to accommodate the difficulties of being a single parent.

You need to give reading and quality time with your kids more importance than just taking care of the housework. Rather than remembering a never-ending list of cleaning-related instructions, these priceless exchanges make enduring memories you wish to treasure.

Being "clean enough" does not entail slacking on basic household upkeep and hygiene. It's critical to maintain dishwashing, tidy up, and do a respectable amount of laundry each week. But family time may take precedence over some less important chores, like matching sock sorting or deep cleaning appliances like the oven.

You have to learn to live with defects in your home if you're a single mother. There are days when having matching socks feels like a luxury, and nothing gets baked. Recognize that these flaws are a fact of life for single parents rather than obsessing over them.

It can be difficult for single mothers to strike a balance between taking care of the house and spending time with their kids. Acknowledging "clean enough" enables us to prioritize meaningful moments, set more reasonable goals, and tolerate the occasional flaw in our houses.

Even though we still practice basic hygiene and cleanliness, we do it with the knowledge that our children's time is incredibly valuable and deserves our attention.

Clean the entire house once a night.

For various compelling reasons, it is imperative for single mothers to complete a general house clean every night. First of all, it keeps the living space tidy and orderly, which directly adds to the feeling of calm and relaxation. This is particularly crucial for single mothers, who already have a lot on their plates.

Maintaining a clutter-free home not only enhances mental health but also provides a good example for the kids.

Nightly cleaning practices can lessen the need for subsequent thorough cleaning sessions by preventing the buildup of dust and filth. Additionally, it creates a cozier atmosphere in the house, which enhances relaxation and family time.

Moreover, having a neat living area guarantees that necessities are easily reached, which saves time and lessens the commotion in the morning.

All things considered, a single mother's life can be greatly improved by developing the habit of cleaning the house every night. It fosters well-being, order, and a sense of accomplishment in keeping the home peaceful.

For single mothers, using a lint roller to clean curtains, lampshades, and other difficult-to-reach spots is a practical and effective tip. Because these places can be challenging to access and fully clean, they are frequently neglected during standard cleaning procedures.

Usually made to remove lint and hair from garments, lint rollers are also a great tool for lampshades and drapes. They efficiently remove dust, pet hair, and other detritus that build up in these areas, greatly enhancing the room's overall appearance and cleanliness right away.

This is a simple and low-effort solution that is perfect for working single mothers who have a lot on their plates and still want to keep their homes clean.

Making use of a lint roller Single mothers may guarantee a more hygienic and comfortable living space in these difficult-to-reach regions without having to devote a lot of time and effort to cleaning, freeing them up to concentrate on other crucial responsibilities.

What are some ways to manage your time?

The instruments, methods, or approaches we use to plan our daily tasks and maximize each minute are known as time management strategies. By using these techniques, we may more effectively manage our time, establish priorities, cut down on lost time, and boost output.

You might think of time management as a jigsaw, with each piece representing a task or activity we need to complete. To get the intended outcome, we must methodically arrange and put together each component, much like in a puzzle. In this instance, the outcome is the accomplishment of our goals and tasks within the allotted time.

From straightforward to-do lists to intricate scheduling and organization systems, there are many different ways to manage time. Among the most popular techniques are the time slot approach and the Pareto principle; choosing and tailoring the plan or methods that best fit our needs and way of life is crucial.

These techniques are frequently successful because they give our days structure, make it easier for us to see our objectives and duties, and aid in maintaining focus. To sum up, time management techniques give us a structure for maximizing our output, reducing our stress levels, and striking a balance between our personal and business obligations.

It's critical to realize that time management techniques aren't made to fit as many tasks into our days as possible. Instead, the goal of these tactics is to make sure we have adequate time for the things that really matter to us. Good time management can help us accomplish our objectives and enhance our quality of life.

Finally, it's important to remember that no time management technique works like magic. The successful application of these tactics necessitates ongoing practice and modification. We must be conscious of how we use our time, evaluate our methods for managing it on a regular basis, and modify our plans as needed. Our capacity for time management has developed in this way as we strive for maximum effectiveness and productivity.

The Time Concept

Time is one of the most basic and fascinating ideas in human understanding; it is sometimes referred to as the fourth dimension. It is a constant, all-encompassing force that regulates the very structure of our lives. Although time appears simple at first glance, its actual essence is much more nuanced and mysterious.

Fundamentally, time is a measure of how events unfold, moving from the past into the present and beyond into the future. It is a constant, unavoidable, and irreversible occurrence that has an impact on all facets of our life. Our sense of time may be incredibly individualized; it can expand or contract based on our feelings, experiences, and environment. Time is an ever-present friend that never stops or reverses course.

Time and space are related in the field of physics, generating the spacetime continuum that is characterized by Albert Einstein's theory of relativity. This idea completely changed the way we think about time by showing that it is relative and depends on one's relative motion and gravity rather than an absolute, universal concept. This groundbreaking realization has profound effects on how we understand the cosmos as a whole.

Another important aspect of the human experience is time. It establishes our daily schedules, affects how we make decisions, and forms our recollections. We arrange our lives according to the passage of time, measuring it in seconds, minutes, hours, and years. Our civilizations, faiths, and philosophical systems are profoundly entwined with the idea of time, which frequently represents the transient nature of life and the necessity of making the most of our time here on Earth.

Beyond human comprehension, time permeates all facets of our existence, from the intimate moments of our own experiences to the physical laws that govern the universe. It is a force that propels us ahead and a reminder of how short life is. It is both continuous and varied. The deep relevance of this mysterious idea in the human journey is highlighted by the way our search to solve its secrets continues to influence our philosophical, scientific, and cultural endeavors.

Chapter 1: Uncovering the Secrets of Efficient Time Management with the Four D's

We must first identify the four essential keys that can unlock your potential for efficient time management before we can begin the journey to mastering time.

Do, Delegate, Defer, and Delete are the four keys that are commonly referred to as "The Four D's." They serve as the cornerstone of an organized strategy for effectively managing your time and duties.

What do these Four D's actually imply, though, and how can you use them to completely change the way you organize your day? To fully comprehend each one's importance and usefulness, let's take a closer look at each one.

Take prompt action.

"D" is first and mainly an abbreviation for "Do." This is the formula's action-oriented component. It's time to get your hands dirty and take on any task or demand that comes up that needs to be done right away.

It is imperative that significant jobs that are also urgent are completed immediately. These are the unanticipated emergencies, the "fires" in your daily life, and the urgent tasks that just can't wait. If you take quick action, you can stop them from getting worse and take more time to solve.

Imagine that your supervisor asks you to submit a report right now because there is a crucial client meeting later on in the day. This is a chore you cannot afford to put off. Under such circumstances, the "Do" principle advises you to give this task top priority and your undivided attention until it is finished.

But it's important to discern between jobs that are actually urgent and those that just seem that way. Occasionally, what appears essential might not be in line with your priorities or long-term objectives. It's critical to assess the task's significance before beginning.

Recall that not every urgent issue is equally important.

Assign: Distributing the Work

A second "D" stands for "Delegate." Envision a group of devoted, competent helpers who can support you in completing your assignments. You can accomplish that without having to dream, though, as delegation is your key to making it happen.

The skill of delegation is giving a job or obligation to someone else who is better or equally qualified to do it. It's about realizing that there are others in your immediate vicinity who can provide their knowledge and abilities and that you don't have to do everything yourself.

Not only does delegation reduce your workload, but it also promotes teamwork and gives others more authority. That's a win-win tactic. You may focus on higher-priority activities with more time and mental capacity when you give up control over some jobs.

Assume you are a manager in charge of a group of workers. You need to analyze your data carefully for a project that you have. A team member with good analytical abilities can be assigned this responsibility to save you hours of poring over spreadsheets. This lets your team member excel in their area of expertise while also saving you time.

But good communication, faith in your teammates, and a readiness to let go of perfectionism are all necessary for effective delegation. Throughout the process, it's critical to offer direction, establish expectations, and keep lines of communication open.

Postpone: Allotted Tasks

This third "D" is for "Defer." There are significant but not necessarily urgent chores that you come upon from time to time. These are the assignments that can be put off until a later period or time.

One smart way to manage your tasks is to defer. It entails realizing that not all tasks must be finished right away and that some are better suited for a later, more convenient time. You may make sure that you use your time and energy more wisely by putting these things off.

Imagine yourself in the position of having a presentation to prepare for a meeting that is still a week away. Even though you should set aside time for this assignment, you don't have to begin working on it immediately. Alternatively, you might postpone it till a later time that better fits into your calendar.

Deferment also includes setting priorities. It involves making the distinction between jobs that, while seemingly urgent, are not really crucial in the long run and those that are. By postponing unimportant chores, you make sure your time is spent where it counts most.

Encouraging Personal Development via Committed Practice: A Story of Physical Proficiency"

John has battled obesity his entire life. He would frequently catch himself skipping his exercise and reaching for junk food. Though he was aware that something needed to change, he was unsure of where to begin.

He was first introduced to the idea of control and discipline in relation to taking care of his physique by a buddy. The notion that he could master his own behavior and responses and that discipline was the means to do so captivated him.

John made the decision to begin modestly and made it his mission to walk for thirty minutes each day. At first, it was challenging because he had to fight the temptation to forgo his daily stroll and eat his favorite foods. However, he persisted through the early difficulties after reminding himself that discipline was essential to reaching his objective.

He saw physical changes as he persisted in following his daily schedule. He experienced weight loss, an increase in vitality, and a boost in self-assurance. Inspired by his own success, John established new objectives for himself, like increasing his weightlifting and cutting back on processed meals.

John experienced difficulties along the way to physical mastery, and there were moments when he considered giving up. However, he never stopped reminding himself of his body's discipline and control, which kept him going.

John was able to change his body and accomplish his goals by exercising control and discipline. He discovered that real power originates from inside and that anyone can attain physical mastery with the correct attitude and willpower.

"The Ability to Control Your Body via Discipline

Everybody wants to be in charge of their bodies. We want to feel good about how we look, be able to move easily, and have the energy to achieve our objectives. But a lot of us have trouble maintaining this sense of control, frequently developing bad habits and putting our physical health last. Discipline is the key to achieving this control.

The capacity to regulate one's behavior and responses in order to accomplish a particular objective is known as discipline. It is the cornerstone of restraint and the secret to realizing our potential. Discipline is crucial for maintaining control over our physical selves. It enables us to withstand temptation, overcome obstacles, and consistently move closer to our objectives.

Establishing a clear and precise aim is the first step towards using discipline to take control of our bodies. This could involve everything from building muscle mass to decreasing weight to enhancing general health. After we have a target in mind, we may create a strategy to get there. This plan ought to outline the precise steps we'll take every day, like exercising, eating right, and taking care of ourselves. Setting a reasonable deadline for accomplishing our objective and keeping in mind the final product we are aiming for is equally crucial.

Achieving success in any aspect of life requires first defining a precise and well-defined aim. Whether in your personal or professional, concentrate your efforts and track your success. In this post, we'll talk about how important it is to have a clear, defined goal and offer advice and techniques for doing so.

Knowing the distinction between a broad and a specific aim is the first step towards creating a clear and precise goal. Something that is vague and wide is called a general goal. One overall objective might be to "get in shape" or "lose weight." These objectives are too vague to offer guidance or a clear idea of what must be done to reach them.

This objective is clear in terms of what needs to be done to get there (reducing 10 pounds), when it will happen (6 months), and how it will be accomplished (three times a week of exercise and a balanced diet).

It's critical to remember the SMART criteria while creating a precise and well-defined goal. The words "specific, measurable, achievable, relevant, and time-bound" are abbreviated as "SMART." A target that fulfills the SMART requirements is one that is:

Specific: The objective should clearly outline what must be accomplished and be well-defined.

Measurable: The objective must have a mechanism for tracking development and identifying success.

Achievable: Considering the available resources and limitations, the objective must be both reasonable and doable.

Relevant: The aim ought to be in line with your main priorities and objectives.

Time-bound: There ought to be a deadline for completing the goal.

It's also critical to remember that defining a precise aim necessitates some introspection. You must be aware of your own priorities, values, and motives in order to establish a clear and precise aim. It is advisable to take into account the limitations and resources at your disposal that could affect your capacity to accomplish the objective.

After deciding on a precise objective, it's critical to develop a plan of action. This strategy must have concrete, quantifiable actions. Together with a schedule for finishing each phase, the plan should also outline how to track development and assess if the objective has been met.

In summary, the first step to success in any endeavor in life is to establish a well-defined and precise goal. You may develop goals that are clear, attainable, and in line with your overall aims and priorities by knowing the distinction between a general and a specific goal and by remembering the SMART criteria. Don't forget to take self-reflection as well, and make a plan of action with a deadline. You can concentrate your efforts, maintain motivation, and track your progress towards accomplishment when you have a well-defined objective in mind.

Improving Intentionality And Observance Of Time

Being mindful of our time and activities has been identified as a critical first step in enhancing our well-being. This awareness can be reached through various techniques, such as gratitude diaries and Vipassana Meditation. For a good reason, mindfulness has become popular in the field of psychology. Dr. Abdul WahabPathath's 2017 study lists a number of advantages of frequent meditation, including lower cholesterol, better oxygen flow, increased creativity, and many more. This is without taking into account the possibility that it will strengthen practitioners' ties to their spiritual heritage.

A 2016 study by Lynda J. Dimitroff et al. discovered that resident nurses greatly benefit by maintaining a straightforward journal. They appeared less worn out and depleted. They also expressed greater levels of enjoyment than they did before writing. The group narrowed down the beneficial benefits to three primary topics. Initially, nurses believed they could share their deepest feelings with others instead of keeping them to themselves. Secondly, they believed they could express and comprehend their emotions. Most essential to us, though, was that participants thought writing helped them make better decisions. After highlighting some of the benefits of these methods, let's examine how they relate to optimizing our time management.

Enhancing Understanding of Time

Psychology has an intriguing stance on time perception. On the one hand, a lot of laypeople are curious about this subject. However, at least initially, the responses it offers can be ambiguous or general. One illustration of how perplexing this may be, even for scientists, is the Theory of Microgenesis. A supporter of the theory said, without delving too further into the matter, that "the mind interprets the sense of time that is so elaborated as a measure of its slow death." Brown (1990)

On less radical studies, nevertheless, we can rely. A University of Tokyo team postulated that raising the pace at which a timer is established could boost worker productivity. It was conceivable that employees would try to meet this new speed unconsciously if this timer was used as a tool to apply artificial pressure. An on-screen timer served as the focal point of the researchers' two-phase investigation on time perception. It had three settings: one that operated normally, one that was slower than usual, and one that was faster. In a five-minute minigame, players had to click on successive objectives. Speed alternated between the three states while the clock stayed in the middle of the screen. It turns out that when the clock moved more slowly, there was a difference of roughly 3% more targets clicking on quickly and a similar drop in speed.

An idea of our changing sense of time that is more easily understood is provided by the aforementioned study. It is probably not unfamiliar to you to feel as though you have been working on an awful chore for hours on end when, in reality, only a few minutes have gone. In a similar vein, even after the majority of our day has passed, it always seems like wonderful things come and go too quickly! This raises a crucial question: How can we exploit our perception of time to further our objectives?

Learning how to estimate time more accurately is a good place to start, though. Timers, similar to those in the study, are a useful tool for this! However, you don't have to change them to move more quickly. It's an easy method to see how much time you have for any particular work. Although there are virtual replicas, the most straightforward substitute is an analog watch. As with most tactics in this book, though, I strongly advise you to modify this to fit your own circumstances.

Journaling or logging is another technique to increase time awareness. An investigation on the subject using the mime app produced some intriguing findings. Whitaker et al. observed that their software, as well as manual records, successfully discouraged users from wasting time on unproductive activities, even though they were unable to increase productive time. With the likelihood of more changes down the road, their tone was upbeat. The researchers considered this awareness and the incentive to repurpose saved time for work to be positive.

This final idea is quite potent. What could be accomplished with more targeted approaches if a basic software that showed time percentages on screen was effective in cutting down on wasted time? An example of a common application of this idea is journaling. You might also choose something simpler, like a rewritten version of the exercise from Chapter 1, in which you recorded every task you completed during the day. This activity has several advantages. First of all, it makes goal-setting stronger. It can also give you a little room to let your feelings out, which will make it easier for you to make cool, collected decisions. Some even discover that journaling allows them to express their artistic or creative side!

Since I had a lot of trouble journaling, I'd also like to share the substitute I used to get the same benefits. I make time every day to do Vipassana Meditation, no matter where I go. This method is quite old, having its roots in India more than 2500 years ago. It was later rediscovered by Gautama Buddha, who included it in the Theravada and Mahayana schools of Buddhism. Beyond any spiritual implications, though, it's a common behavior among individuals of different faiths. There are numerous fitness applications with a meditation mode. Some even offer guided meditations and a number of articles outlining the "perfect" practice for each objective.

Even with all of these complexities, I participate in a far more basic form. I'll schedule a fifteen-minute time slot in which I'll sit comfortably and pay close attention to my breathing. I'll accept that thoughts, feelings, and sounds are common and then return my focus to my breathing. Please search for a video on it and give it a shot. After some time has gone, if meditation still interests you, I suggest trying it out regularly for a month. This will ensure that you get to personally feel the benefits of the procedure.

Let us now discuss another contentious issue: procrastination. It was especially difficult for me to get over this obstacle. Prior to taking control of my own time, I used to spend a lot of time either procrastinating or, in certain really odd cases, avoiding procrastination by engaging in other pointless activities that were "technically a task." Let's examine the actions we may take on a daily basis to reduce time waste.

Work-Life Balance And Stress Reduction

Action plan: Develop strategies for managing stress and arranging a work-life balance.

Your attempts to live a balanced life that includes effective stress management and a healthy work-life balance will determine your overall health. This action plan will guide you through the process of developing stress-reduction techniques and assist you in striking a healthy work-life balance.

Take some time to identify the precise pressures in your life. These could have to do with business, personal matters, or both.

Understanding How Stress Impacts You

Find out how stress affects the body and mind negatively. Understanding the potential damage to your health is the first step towards taking control of it.

The Link Between the Body and Mind:

Realize the close connection between your body and mind. Understand how stress affects your body because it can result in physical problems.

Techniques for Reducing Stress

Use deep breathing techniques, such as the 4-7-8 method or diaphragmatic breathing, to calm your body and mind.

Zen and mindfulness

Frequent physical activity

Exercise frequently to release endorphins, which are your body's natural way of reducing stress.

Time Management:

Employ effective time management strategies to reduce the stress of deadlines and increase output.

Finding the Work-Life Balance

Establish Boundaries:

Make clear distinctions between your personal and work lives. Turn off work-related alerts while not in use.

Prioritize taking care of yourself:

Make self-care a priority in your everyday activities. This includes things like reading, taking a bath, or just passing the time.

Effective Time Management:

Make time every week for your personal, professional, and familial interests. As closely as you can, adhere to your plan.

Delegate and outsource:

Assigning responsibilities at work and home shouldn't be a problem. Frequent Check-Ins: Think about outsourcing your errands or chores to give yourself extra time.

Assess your work-life balance on a regular basis. It can be necessary to modify your schedule and priorities in order to maintain balance.

Strategies for Achieving Work-Life Harmony

Priority of Quality: Pay attention to the caliber of your time rather than just how many hours you spend with your family and at work.

People closest to you:

These ties can provide emotional support when times are hard.

Setting Realistic Goals

Set realistic goals for both your personal and professional lives. Unrealistic expectations might lead to burnout.

Digital withdrawal

Periodically disconnect from devices to refuel yourself and spend uninterrupted time with loved ones.

Savour the Present: Practice mindfulness by being totally present in the moment, whether you're with your family or at work.

Say No Often: When your schedule is already packed, graciously decline new commitments. Saying no is a part of self-care.

Accept Your Imperfection:

Without casting judgment, accept the imperfections in your life and in yourself.

Celebrate small victories:

No matter how small, be proud of and acknowledge your achievements. This lowers stress and boosts optimism.

Make contact with supportive networks:

To discuss your feelings and experiences, establish or seek out support networks with friends, family, or support groups.

Finding a good work-life balance and becoming an expert at managing stress take time, but the journey is worthwhile for your physical and emotional well-being. By identifying the sources of stress in your life, putting stress reduction strategies to use, and creating work-life balance plans, you may lead a productive and fulfilling existence.

Remember that everyone has a different definition of balance. As you go along this path, keep an open mind and be willing to try new things since what works for you might not work for someone else. You can achieve the illusive balance that so many individuals in today's busy world are looking for by making conscious decisions to maintain your mental health and giving self-care first priority.

In the end, attaining a work-life balance requires more than just managing stress and finding a stable balance; it also requires living a life that is consistent with your values, brings you joy, and helps you to thrive both personally and professionally.

3. The Head's Function in Time Management

How to Create a Productive Team and Lead by Example.

In addition to overseeing your personal schedule, time management as a business owner entails inspiring and guiding your staff to reach their greatest potential. We'll talk about the importance of leadership in time management in this chapter, as well as how to set a positive example for your team and foster productivity.

1. Set a good example

The foundation of efficient time management is leadership. It's crucial for a leader to set an example for the behaviors they desire from their team members. This entails exhibiting efficient time management techniques, such as showing up on time for meetings, setting priorities for your most important work, and assigning duties to others.

2. Express Your Expectations Evidently

Having clear communication is essential to time management success. Make sure everyone in your team is aware of their roles' expectations and obligations. Assign tasks with precise due dates and give regular feedback to make sure everyone is working towards the same goals.

3. Offer Guidance and Assistance

Not every team member will possess the same degree of proficiency in managing their time. Give your team members the guidance and assistance they need to acquire the time management skills they require. This could be one-on-one coaching, time management seminars, or access to tools and applications for productivity.

4. Honour and Commend Achievements

Time management that works takes work and commitment. Acknowledge and praise team members who accomplish their goals and show effective time management. This might foster a positive work atmosphere and inspire your staff.

5. Encourage a Productivity Culture

Establishing a productive culture helps support your team's motivation and attention. Promote cooperation and teamwork, and commemorate victories together as a group. Establish hard but attainable objectives and monitor advancement often to make sure everyone is moving in the right direction.

6. Promote a balanced work-life

Urge the members of your team to prioritize their mental health, take well-deserved breaks, and strike a healthy work-life balance. Increased productivity and job satisfaction may result from this.

Actual Cases:

1. Set a Good Example: As a business owner, you can set a good example for

your employees by managing your time well. To show your team how to manage their time well, you might assign duties to others, prioritize your tasks wisely, and show up on time for meetings.

2. Express Your Expectations Clearly: To make sure your team members are aware of their duties and deadlines, you can make sure you express your expectations to them in a clear and concise manner. To make sure everyone is on track, you can, for instance, assign assignments with deadlines, give verbal or written directions, and schedule frequent check-ins.

3. Offer Training and assistance: To assist your team members in acquiring time management skills, you can offer them Training and assistance. For instance, you may hold time management seminars, give out tools or applications for productivity, and give team members who require more support one-on-one coaching.

4. Acknowledge and recognize Achievements: You can recognize team members who show excellent time management skills and accomplish their objectives. As an example, you can inspire and uplift others by publicly praising team members' achievements, giving verbal or written praise, or providing incentives or awards.

5. Promote a Productive Culture: You may encourage a productive culture in your group or company. To build a productive work atmosphere, you might, for instance, reward cooperation and teamwork, set ambitious but attainable goals, monitor progress frequently, and celebrate victories as a group.

6. Promote Work-Life Balance: You may motivate the people on your team to keep a positive work-life balance. In order to guarantee that team members have time for their personal life, you might, for instance, prioritize mental health and well-being, encourage breaks during the workday, provide flexible work schedules, and set boundaries. All

of these actions can boost productivity and job satisfaction.

www.ingramcontent.com/pod-product-compliance
Lightning Source LLC
Chambersburg PA
CBHW052143110526
44591CB00012B/1839